MAKING THE PLAY

BASEBALL

BY VALERIE BODDEN

CREATIVE EDUCATION · CREATIVE PAPERBACKS

Published by Creative Education and Creative Paperbacks
P.O. Box 227, Mankato, Minnesota 56002
Creative Education and Creative Paperbacks
are imprints of The Creative Company
www.thecreativecompany.us

Design and production by The Design Lab
Art direction by Rita Marshall
Printed in the United States of America

Photographs by iStockphoto (t_kimura), Shutterstock
(AkeSak, Brocreative, Beto Chagas, Adrian Coroama,
kitzcorner, Mega Pixel, tammykayphoto, Todd
Taulman, tonyz20, Tom Wang, Jan de Wild)

Library of Congress Cataloging-in-Publication Data
Bodden, Valerie.
Baseball / Valerie Bodden.
p. cm. — (Making the play)
Includes index.
Summary: An elementary introduction to the physics involved
in the sport of baseball, including scientific concepts such as
momentum and trajectory, and actions such as pitching and batting.
ISBN 978-1-60818-653-2 (hardcover)
ISBN 978-1-62832-232-3 (pbk)
ISBN 978-1-56660-684-4 (eBook)
1. Baseball—Juvenile literature. 2. Physics—Juvenile literature. I. Title.

GV867.5.B64 2016
796.357—dc23   2015007569

CCSS: RI.1.1, 2, 3, 4, 5, 6, 7; RI.2.1, 2, 3, 5, 6, 7,
10; RI.3.1, 3, 5, 7, 8; RF.2.3, 4; RF.3.3

First Edition HC 9 8 7 6 5 4 3 2 1
First Edition PBK 9 8 7 6 5 4 3 2 1

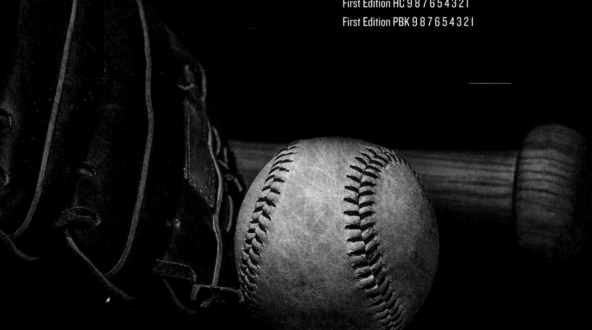

CONTENTS

BASEBALL AND SCIENCE

The baseball whizzes toward home plate.

You swing. *Crack!* The ball flies off the bat.

It's a home run!

HOME RUN!

Do you think about science when you play baseball? Probably not. But you use science anyway. A science called physics (*FIZ-icks*) can help you swing, pitch, and throw. Let's see how!

SWEET SPOT

When you hit a baseball with a bat, the bat shakes. Think of it like a plucked guitar string. Some of the bat's **energy** is wasted when it shakes.

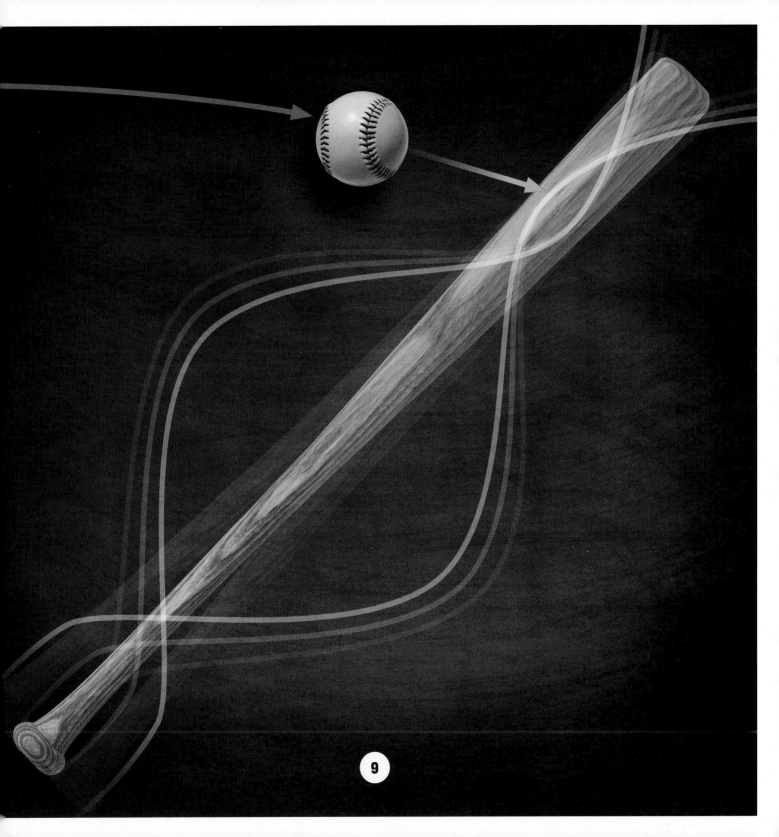

One area on the bat does not shake.

This is called the "sweet spot."

You want to hit the ball at the sweet spot. Then the bat won't shake as much. The ball will get more energy. It will go farther!

Four to 7 inches (10.2–17.8 cm) from the end of a 30-inch (76.2 cm) bat

SWEET SPOT

MOMENTUM

Have you ever studied a baseball pitcher? He uses his whole body to throw. First he turns and lifts his knee to his chest. Then he takes a step. His shoulder, arm, and hand move forward. These actions create **momentum**.

Bigger and faster-moving objects have more momentum. The pitcher's body **transfers** speed to the ball when he lets go. The pitcher might make the ball spin. Spin can make the ball curve and drop.

TRAJECTORY

The path of something
moving through the air

Stepping forward can help you pitch better. Where else could you use momentum in baseball? How about when you run to catch a fly ball? Give it a try, and make the play!

MOMENTUM ON THE MOVE

Momentum is affected by speed and **mass**.

WHAT YOU NEED

- 2 toy cars, one heavier than the other
- A ramp

Place both cars at the top of the ramp. Let go of them at the same time. Which one was faster? Which traveled farther? What does this tell you about the cars' momentum? Now give the lighter car a push down the ramp. Let the heavier car down the ramp at the same time, but don't push it. How does changing the lighter car's speed change its momentum? Can you get the lighter car to go farther than the heavier car?

GLOSSARY

energy-the ability to do work, or apply a push or a pull to move an object

mass-the amount of material that makes up an object

momentum-a measure of an object's movement based on its mass and how fast it is moving

transfers-passes from one thing to another

READ MORE

Bourassa, Barbara. *Bat and Ball Sports*.
North Mankato, Minn.: QEB, 2007.

Gore, Bryson. *Physics*. Mankato, Minn.: Stargazer, 2009.

Walton, Ruth. *Let's Go to the Playground*.
Mankato, Minn.: Sea-to-Sea, 2013.

WEBSITES

DragonflyTV: Baseball
http://pbskids.org/dragonflytv /show/baseball.html
Watch a video to learn more about a bat's sweet spot.

Science of Baseball
http://www.exploratorium.edu /baseball/
See if you're quick enough to hit a fastball and learn how to throw different pitches.

NOTE: Every effort has been made to ensure that the websites listed above are suitable for children, that they have educational value, and that they contain no inappropriate material. However, because of the nature of the Internet, it is impossible to guarantee that these sites will remain active indefinitely or that their contents will not be altered.

INDEX